We Love Holidays

Celebrating Holi: A Hindu Celebration of Spring

Sujatha Menon

PowerKiDS press

New York

Published in 2009 by The Rosen Publishing Group Inc.
29 East 21st Street, New York, NY 10010

First Edition

Series Editor: Jean Coppendale
Senior Design Manager: Simmi Sikka
Designer: Diksha Khatri

Library of Congress Cataloging-in-Publication Data

Menon, Sujatha.
  Celebrating Holi : a Hindu celebration of spring / Sujatha Menon. – 1st ed.
      p. cm. – (We love holidays)
  Includes index.
  ISBN 978-1-4358-2843-8 (library binding)
  ISBN 978-1-4358-2903-9 (paperback.)
  ISBN 978-1-4358-2907-7 (6-pack)
  1. Holi (Hindu festival)–Juvenile literature. I. Title.
  BL1239.82.H65M46 2009
  294.5'36–dc22
                                        2008030371

Manufactured in China

The publishers would like to thank the following for allowing us to reproduce their pictures in this book:
REUTERS: title page, 4, Raj Patidar; 21, Kamal Kishore; 22, Stringer India / Preston Merchant: 5 / Bhaktivedanta Book Trust International, Inc. www.krishna.com: 6 / Alamy: 7, 10, ArkReligion.com; 12, Tim Gainey / THE HINDU: 8, 9, 14, 15, 23 / epa: cover, 11, Manjunath Kiran / Stephen Knapp: 13 / His Divine Grace A C Bhaktivedant Swami Prabhupada: 16 / wildphotos.com: 17, Anil Dev / Karun Thakur: 18 / Lonely Planet Images: 19, Greg Elms / IndiaPicture: 20, 21.

Contents

Web Sites
Due to the changing nature of Internet links, PowerKids Press has developed an online list of Web sites related to the subject of this book. This site is updated regularly. Please use this link to access this list: www.powerkidslinks.com/wlh/holi

A shopkeeper in India sells brightly colored powders, which people throw at each other during Holi.

Hoorah! Holi is here!

Holi is a popular Hindu festival. It is celebrated on the day of the **full Moon** in March.

Hindus celebrate Holi to welcome the arrival of spring. They celebrate with colored powder and water, music, dance, and lots of tasty things to eat.

Children in New York take part in a Holi parade. These parades are popular among Hindu children around the world.

DID YOU KNOW?

On the day of Holi, Hindu farmers offer prayers for a good harvest by roasting grains of wheat in a fire.

Good against evil

Prahlad tells his friends to have faith in God, since He will always help those who believe in Him.

Holi celebrates the victory of good over evil. In Hindu **legend**, there once lived a bad king named Hiranyakashyap, who ordered his people to worship him as God. But his son, Prahlad, believed in the real God. The king grew angry and told his sister, Holika, to kill Prahlad.

Holika had special powers that stopped her from getting burned, so she sat in a **bonfire** with Prahlad. But God took away her powers because she was using them for evil. Holika died, but Prahlad was saved.

Children in London, U.K., take part in a play about Holika and Prahlad. Plays such as this help children to learn more about the festival of Holi.

Small Holi

Holi lasts for two days in most countries, except for Nepal, where it is celebrated for a whole week. The first day is called *choti holi* (small Holi). On this day, people clean their houses and collect broken furniture and pieces of wood.

Hindus in India prepare to light their street bonfire.

At night, people pile up the wood outside their homes and set it on fire.

A mannequin of Holika is placed in the bonfire to mark the victory of good over evil.

DID YOU KNOW?

In some countries, such as Surinam and Trinidad and Tobago, people burn a castor oil plant instead of lighting bonfires.

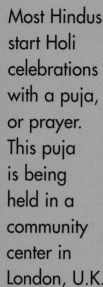

Most Hindus start Holi celebrations with a puja, or prayer. This puja is being held in a community center in London, U.K.

Festival of colors

Everyone waits excitedly for the day after small Holi. This is the day when people from all religions and ages come together to have fun.

People wear old clothes and go out into the streets to throw colored powder and water at each other. It is very exciting for children, since they are allowed to play tricks on the adults.

DID YOU KNOW?

Many Hindus who do not live in India meet in community centers and temples to celebrate Holi.

Covering each other with colored powder or water is the most enjoyable part of Holi for children.

11

Holi and Krishna

A young boy dressed as Krishna for Holi. Krishna often played the flute to calm Radha when she was angered by his tricks.

The colored powder used in Holi also has a story attached to it. It is said that Krishna was **jealous** of his good friend, Radha, because of her light-colored skin.

Krishna playing Holi with Radha and her friends.

So one day, Krishna's mother told him to paint Radha's face. Krishna threw colored powder on Radha and her friends. Now we do this every year.

13

Bathed in color

Some Hindus spray colored water at each other using water pistols. Children throw balloons filled with colored water.

Children love to spray colored water at each other using *pichkari*, or water pistols.

In other places, colored powder is mixed in swimming pools. People enjoy taking a dip in these colored pools.

People have fun throwing colored water at each other. But the colors mixed in water are difficult to wash off.

Holi in Krishna's land

Some Hindus decorate models of Krishna and Radha with silk clothes and gold jewelry.

In many countries, Holi celebrates the life of Lord Krishna. Hindus in Bangladesh take out figures of Krishna and Radha in a grand **procession**.

Mathura, a small city in northern India, is believed to be Krishna's birthplace. Here, Holi celebrations last for two weeks.

People from all over the world come to Mathura during Holi, to join in the celebrations.

DID YOU KNOW?

Some Hindus put up a decorated pole. This is supposed to be the tree where Krishna used to hide after playing tricks on Radha.

Holi feast

Sweets are a major part of many Indian festivals. On Holi, some Hindu women make a special sweet food called **gujiya**, which is eaten at big family parties.

Hindu children in Delhi, India, enjoying a delicious snack of *gujiyas*.

Thandai is another important part of the celebration. This is a special, flavored milk with watermelon seeds, almonds, cashews, and **cardamom** seeds added.

Lots of other delicious foods, such as a flat bread called *puri* and fried potatoes, are made on Holi.

Along the streets

Holi is celebrated in many different ways by Hindus around the world. Music and dance are a big part of the celebrations both inside and outside of India.

The elephant festival in Rajasthan takes place every year during Holi.

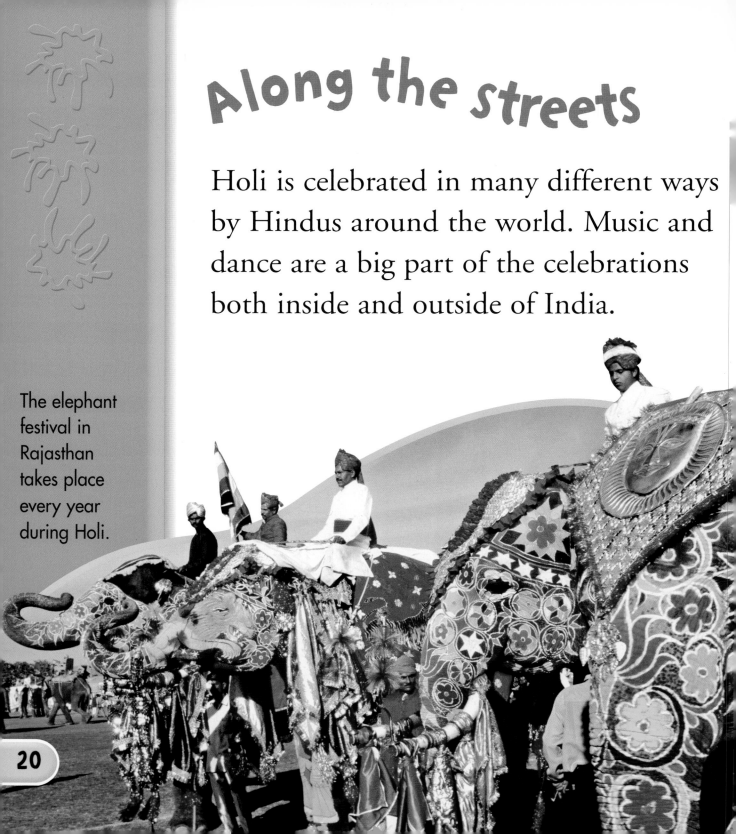

In India, people dance in the streets to the beat of the *dhol*, an Indian drum. Colorful parades take place in many big cities.

People wearing traditional clothes dance through the streets of Rajasthan in India.

DID YOU KNOW?

Holi is a holiday that is celebrated in many countries where lots of Hindus live, such as Guyana and Nepal.

A greener Holi

Actors throw flowers during a play about Holi. Many people now throw flowers instead of colored powder.

Most of the colored powder used today is harmful to the skin and eyes. So many people have started using different materials.

A mannequin of Holika, decorated with lights.

Some Hindus in India do not burn large bonfires in the streets, because this can be dangerous. So instead, they decorate figures of Holika with lights. The lights make the figures look as if they are burning, but are much safer.

23

Index and further information

GLOSSARY

bonfire a large fire that is built outside by piling up wood

cardamom a herb that is found in India, the seeds of which are added to food to make it taste better

full Moon the day on which we can see the complete disk of the Moon from Earth

gujiya a crescent-shaped Indian sweet food that is filled with grated coconut, raisins, and sugar syrup

jealous a feeling of dislike for someone because they have something that we long for

legend a story that is so old that no one knows who first told it

procession a large group of people walking in a line, sometimes singing and dancing to the beat of drums or other instruments

BOOKS TO READ

Here Comes Holi: The Festival of Colors by Meenal Pandya (MeeRa Publications, 2003)

Hinduism (World Religions) by Ranchor Prime (Walrus Books, 2005)

Holi (Rookie Read-About Holidays) by Uma Krishnaswami (Children's Press, 2003)